Lightning
Revised Edition

by Erin Edison
Consulting Editor: Gail Saunders-Smith, PhD

CAPSTONE PRESS
a capstone imprint

Pebble Plus is published by Capstone Press,
1710 Roe Crest Drive, North Mankato, Minnesota 56003.
www.capstonepub.com

Copyright © 2012 by Capstone Press, a Capstone imprint. All rights reserved.

No part of this publication may be reproduced in whole or in part, or stored in a retrieval system, or transmitted in any form or by any means, electronic, mechanical, photocopying, recording, or otherwise, without written permission of the publisher. For information regarding permission, write to Capstone Press, 1710 Roe Crest Drive, North Mankato, Minnesota 56003.

Library of Congress Cataloging-in-Publication Data
Edison, Erin.
  Lightning / by Erin Edison.
     p. cm.—(Pebble plus. Weather basics)
  Summary: "Simple text and full-color photographs describe lightning and how it forms"—Provided by publisher.
  Includes bibliographical references and index.
  ISBN 978-1-6690-2066-0 (revised paperback)
  1. Lightning—Juvenile literature. I. Title. II. Series.
  QC966.5.E35 2012
  551.56'32—dc22   2010053977

Editorial Credits
Erika L. Shores, editor; Kyle Grenz, designer; Laura Manthe, production specialist

Photo Credits
Alamy: Horizon International Images Limited, 11; Getty Image: Minerva Studio, 17, AJ Schroetlin/500px, 19, dimabl, 13, PASPhotography, 21; Shutterstock: Andraž Cerar, back cover, James "BO" Insogna, cover, Jhaz Photography, 1, 5, 7, 15, marcus55, design element, valdezrl, 9

Capstone Press thanks Mike Shores, earth science teacher at RBA Public Charter School in Mankato, Minnesota, for his assistance on this book.

Note to Parents and Teachers

The Weather Basics series supports national science standards related to earth science. This book describes and illustrates lightning. The images support early readers in understanding the text. The repetition of words and phrases helps early readers learn new words. This book also introduces early readers to subject-specific vocabulary words, which are defined in the Glossary section. Early readers may need assistance to read some words and to use the Table of Contents, Glossary, Read More, Internet Sites, and Index sections of the book.

Table of Contents

What Is Lightning? 4
Kinds of Lightning 12
Crash and Boom 18
Stay Safe 20

Glossary. 22
Read More. 23
Internet Sites. 23
Index. 24

What Is Lightning?

Bright flashes light up the sky.

Big jagged streaks hit the ground.

A summer storm has

brought lightning.

Lightning is a kind of electricity.
Storm clouds carry water droplets and ice crystals. The tiny particles bump into one another.
They make electricity in the clouds.

As the electricity becomes stronger, lightning flashes. Lightning is how clouds get rid of electricity.

Lines of lightning are called bolts. They can be 10 miles (16 kilometers) long. They can be 54,000 degrees Fahrenheit (30,000 degrees Celsius).

Kinds of Lightning

Ribbon lightning looks like jagged streaks. It darts from the sky toward the ground.

Forked lightning also goes from a cloud toward the ground. It looks like an upside-down tree.

Lightning doesn't always shoot toward the ground. Sheet lightning streaks inside a cloud. Lightning bolts also jump from cloud to cloud.

Crash and Boom

Thunder is the sound of lightning heating the air. A loud crash means lightning is close. Many booms mean lightning is far away.

Stay Safe

Lightning is dangerous.

Stay indoors during thunderstorms.

If you're caught outside during a storm, stay away from trees and power lines.

Glossary

bolt—a line of lightning coming out of a cloud

electricity—a form of energy caused by moving particles

particle—a tiny piece of something

thunder—the sound made when lightning heats the air

Read More

Flanagan, Alice K. *Thunder and Lightning.* Weather Watch. Mankato, Minn.: Child's World, Inc., 2010.

Goldsmith, Mike. *The Weather.* Now We Know About. New York: Crabtree Pub., 2010.

Salas, Laura Purdie. *Colors of Weather.* Colors All Around. Mankato, Minn.: Capstone Press, 2011.

Internet Sites

FactHound offers a safe, fun way to find Internet sites related to this book. All of the sites on FactHound have been researched by our staff.

Here's all you do:

Visit *www.facthound.com*

Type in this code: 9781429660587

Check out projects, games and lots more at *www.capstonekids.com*

Index

bolts, 10, 16
clouds, 6, 8, 14, 16
electricity, 6, 8
forked lightning, 14
ice crystals, 6
particles, 6
power lines, 20

ribbon lightning, 12
safety, 20
sheet lightning, 16
storms, 4, 6, 20
thunder, 18
trees, 20
water droplets, 6

Word Count: 178
Grade: 1
Early-Intervention Level: 18